EDGE
BOOKS™

WARRIORS OF HISTORY

GREEN BERETS

by Jason Glaser

Consultant:
James O. Gregory
Major, Special Forces
U.S. Army Special Forces Command
(Airborne)

Capstone
press ®

Mankato, Minnesota

Edge Books are published by Capstone Press,
151 Good Counsel Drive, P.O. Box 669, Mankato, Minnesota 56002.
www.capstonepress.com

Library of Congress Cataloging-in-Publication Data
Glaser, Jason.
  Green Berets / by Jason Glaser.
  p. cm.—(Edge Books. Warriors of History)
  Includes bibliographical references and index.
  ISBN-13: 978-0-7368-6430-5 (hardcover)
  ISBN-10: 0-7368-6430-X (hardcover)
  1. United States. Army. Special Forces—Juvenile literature. I. Title. II. Series.
UA34.S64G53 2007
356'.1670973—dc22   2005034935

Summary: Describes the Green Berets, including their history, weapons,
  and way of life.

Editorial Credits

Mandy Robbins, editor; Thomas Emery, designer; Cynthia Martin, illustrator;
  Kim Brown, production artist; Jo Miller, photo researcher; Scott Thoms,
  photo editor

Photo Credits

AP/Wide World Photos, cover, 8-9, 11; Al Jacinto, 12; Laurent Rebours,
  15; Wally Santana, 18; Brennan Linsley, 29
Corbis, 6–7; Bettmann, 24
Courtesy of the Alamo Scout Association, 4
Courtesy of U.S. Army Special Forces Command (Airborne), 14, 22–23, 28
Getty Images Inc./Spencer Platt, 27; Time Life Pictures/Mai Mai/Greg
  Mathieson, 7
John F. Kennedy Library, 10
U.S. Army Photo by SSG Amanda C. Glenn, 16–17

1 2 3 4 5 6 11 10 09 08 07 06

TABLE OF CONTENTS

CHAPTER 1
BEHIND-THE-SCENES FIGHTERS

LEARN ABOUT:
- World War II
- The Soviet threat
- A symbol of pride

The Alamo Scouts completed more than 100 missions behind enemy lines and never lost a single man.

Between 1939 and 1945, World War II raged around the world. Tanks rumbled across Europe. Fighter planes soared over the Pacific Ocean. Bombs fell from the sky. Working together, the United States and their allies defeated Germany, Italy, and Japan.

INVISIBLE HEROES

World War II was fought like many wars before it. Soldiers fought with tanks, planes, and guns. Huge armies took over or freed cities held by the other side.

The United States and their allies also had small groups of soldiers making a big impact. The groups had names like the "Alamo Scouts" and "Devil's Brigade." They performed special operations behind enemy lines and trained local citizens to fight. Together, the soldiers and citizens freed many parts of Europe and Asia from Germany, Japan, and Italy.

EDGE FACT ⊗ ⊗ ⊗ ⊗

From 1866 to 1947, American Indians served in the U.S. Army as scouts behind enemy lines. Indian Scouts earned Medals of Honor in almost every U.S. operation in the 1800s and early 1900s.

Troop "B" Oglala Indian Scouts

Small groups of soldiers had fought behind the scenes in every war America had been in. But it wasn't until World War II that there was special training for them. The new training program was a huge success. Unfortunately, when the war was over, government officials shut down the program.

The crossed arrows on the Green Beret
logo honor the Indian Scouts.

BIRTH OF THE GREEN BERETS

After World War II, the Soviet Union became a very powerful country. The U.S. government began having political disagreements with the Soviets. Americans feared the Soviet Union might attack them.

*In the early 1960s, Special Forces soldiers trained
for missions in the woods of West Virginia.*

The U.S. government wanted to protect the
country from the Soviets. In 1952, the Army
started training soldiers to work behind enemy
lines again. Many of the soldiers had fought in
World War II. These men called themselves U.S.
Army Special Forces soldiers.

In 1962, President Kennedy called the green beret "a symbol of excellence, a badge of courage, a mark of distinction in the fight for freedom."

With President Kennedy's support, the green beret became an official part of the Special Forces uniform.

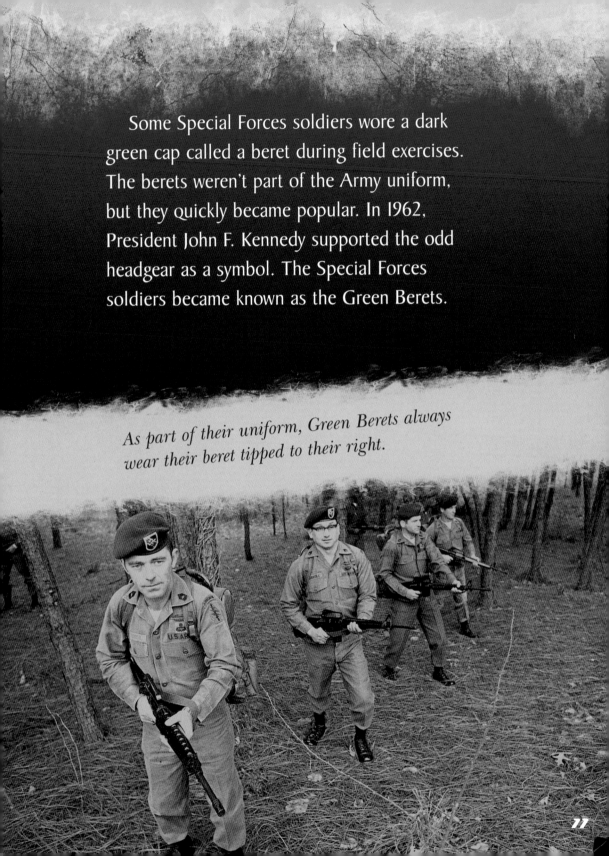

Some Special Forces soldiers wore a dark green cap called a beret during field exercises. The berets weren't part of the Army uniform, but they quickly became popular. In 1962, President John F. Kennedy supported the odd headgear as a symbol. The Special Forces soldiers became known as the Green Berets.

As part of their uniform, Green Berets always wear their beret tipped to their right.

CHAPTER II
SPECIAL FORCES TRAINING

LEARN ABOUT:

- Qualifications
- Intense training
- The final test

Green Berets must learn how to operate more types of weapons than other Army soldiers.

Not everyone can be a Green Beret.
The military only accepts male U.S. citizens
between 20 and 30 years old. Candidates are
usually already in the military. They must be
highly intelligent and in top physical shape.
Green Berets must also learn to speak another
language fluently.

Although many female soldiers have
these qualifications, they can't be Green
Berets. Green Berets teach troops in many
countries. People in some other countries
don't consider women to be equals. Men in
these countries wouldn't take orders from a
female soldier.

TRAINING

During training, recruits work alone in a testing area for days at a time. They must find their own food and shelter. Recruits map their way around unfamiliar land while avoiding other soldiers who are chasing them. They may have to walk or run for miles. Recruits may also have to carry bags of sand to feel what it is like to carry wounded soldiers.

Recruits learn how to fight in many types of terrain, including sandy beaches.

Learning how to parachute is an important part of Green Beret training.

On missions, Green Berets are at high risk for capture. They must steer clear of the enemy. Soldiers learn to use parachutes to enter enemy territory at night. This allows them to enter a country unnoticed by the enemy.

During Robin Sage, recruits act like Green Berets would in a real combat situation.

A recruit's final test is called "Robin Sage." Soldiers are put into groups of 12, as they would be on a real mission. These teams are tested in an area near Fort Bragg, North Carolina. Other soldiers and local citizens enact a fake war between "Pineland" and "The United Province of Atlantica."

The "Pinelanders" test recruits. They set up
situations that could happen on a real mission. Using
their physical and mental skills, recruits do their best
to pass these tests. Soldiers who pass Robin Sage can
become Green Berets.

CHAPTER III
A DIFFERENT KIND OF SOLDIER

LEARN ABOUT:

- A Green Beret's greatest strength
- Peaceful duties
- Weapons

Green Berets modify their uniforms. In desert climates, they wear light clothing.

Green Berets don't think or act like other soldiers. They don't have regular marches, drills, or routine inspections. Both officers and enlisted men share the "grunt work" usually given to lower-ranking soldiers. Green Berets want to be told what to do, but not how to do it. They find their own ways to succeed.

A Green Beret's greatest strength is his creativity. Green Berets work in small groups with limited equipment in remote areas. Often, they must find creative solutions to problems.

Green Berets must find out what enemies are doing. Then, they have to stop them. Green Berets may try to ruin enemy operations, attack enemies directly, or capture enemy leaders.

Beret
Green Berets are one of the few select groups in the Army that do not wear a black beret.

Rifle
The M-4 Carbine rifle is the gun most commonly used by Green Berets.

Pockets
Green Berets carry extra ammunition and tools in their many pockets.

Holster
Green Berets keep sidearms in holsters.

Combat boots
Special Forces soldiers wear boots that are shock-absorbant and water-resistant.

WORKING WITH LOCAL PEOPLE

Green Berets often train local villagers to fight. Green Berets are skilled at a type of fighting called guerilla warfare. Guerilla warfare helps small groups fight much larger groups. It includes setting traps, using surprise attacks, and destroying enemy weapons or defenses.

Most missions also involve helping local people. Green Berets bring food to poor villagers. Medics provide medicine and treat the sick. The teams' engineers help build waterways or bridges for local farmers. Green Berets may even set up schools to teach local people.

The Green Berets' peace-keeping missions are important because they build good relationships. Local people can provide important information about an area. They may also give Green Berets weapons and supplies. Without help from locals, Green Berets couldn't continue their missions.

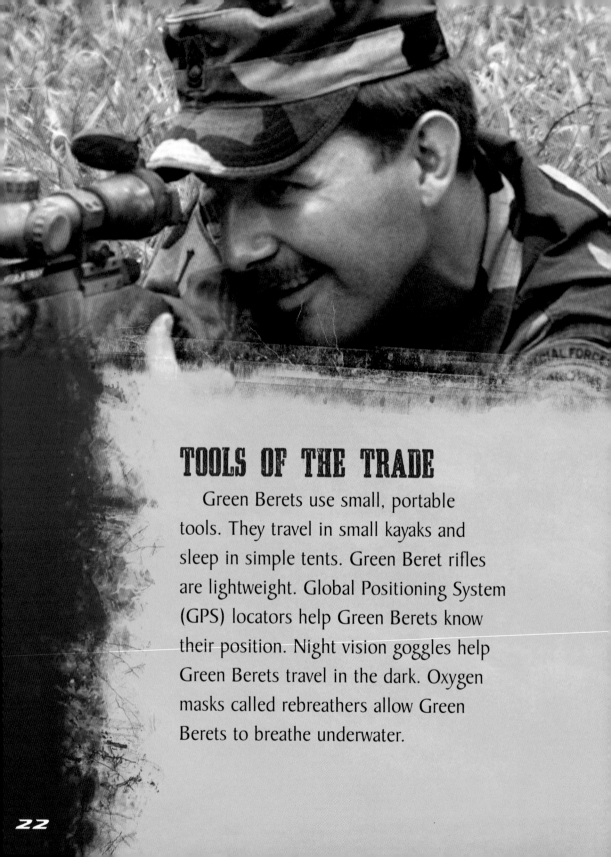

TOOLS OF THE TRADE

Green Berets use small, portable
tools. They travel in small kayaks and
sleep in simple tents. Green Beret rifles
are lightweight. Global Positioning System
(GPS) locators help Green Berets know
their position. Night vision goggles help
Green Berets travel in the dark. Oxygen
masks called rebreathers allow Green
Berets to breathe underwater.

Scopes help Green Berets see what enemies are doing from far away.

Green Berets also use their creativity to make or find weapons. They use what is available to them. A rake or a shovel could be a weapon. The guns Green Berets carry can often use ammunition provided by locals or captured from the enemy.

CHAPTER IV

GREEN BERETS IN ACTION

LEARN ABOUT:
- Green Berets in Vietnam
- Fighting terrorism
- Green Berets today

In Vietnam, Green Berets risked their lives to make sure none of their men were left behind.

During the Vietnam War (1954–1975), Green Berets learned that American prisoners were being tortured at a camp called Son Tay. A group of 56 Green Berets made their way through an area patrolled by about 230,000 enemy soldiers. The Green Berets killed about 300 guards. They broke through the camp's defenses and escaped without losing a single man.

Unfortunately, enemy soldiers had already moved the prisoners, so the Green Berets could not rescue them. But the attack scared the North Vietnamese soldiers. They began treating prisoners better. The prisoners gained new hope from knowing someone tried to rescue them.

MODERN MISSIONS

After the Vietnam War, the United States began to recognize a new threat. By the 1980s, acts of terrorism were increasing throughout the world. Terrorists usually operated in small groups and moved often. A few terrorists could attack a building, plane, or ship, killing many people. A regular army couldn't fight these enemies.

On September 11, 2001, terrorists killed thousands of Americans. They hijacked airplanes and slammed them into the World Trade Center and the Pentagon. For many Green Berets, the attacks were a call to action.

EDGE FACT ⊚ ⊚ ⊚ ⊚

The Green Berets' motto is "De Oppresso Liber." It is Latin for "Free the Oppressed." It reminds them of their duty to help friendly countries and civilians endangered by enemy forces.

The September 11th attacks marked the start of a new kind of war—a war against terrorism.

Today, Green Berets are located all over the world. Many are in the Middle East, looking for the people who plan terrorist attacks. Green Berets have helped destroy terrorist training camps. They also captured people who trained terrorists.

Green Berets respect the customs and cultures of the local people they work with.

Green Berets in Afghanistan must earn the trust of local people so they can work together to fight terrorism.

Wherever they go, Green Berets bring hope to civilians. They capture weapons and terrorists before anyone is hurt. By placing themselves in danger, Green Berets help keep others safe.

GLOSSARY

allies (AL-eyes)—people, groups, or countries that work together for a common cause

engineer (en-juh-NIHR)—someone who designs and builds machines or structures

guerilla warfare (gur-RIL-lah WOR-fair)—a type of military action using small groups of soldiers to carry out surprise attacks against enemy forces

hijack (HYE-jak)—to take illegal control of a vehicle

kayak (KYE-ak)—a covered, narrow boat that holds one person

terrorist (TER-uhr-ist)—someone who uses violence and threats to frighten people into obeying

READ MORE

Green, Michael, and Gladys Green. *Green Berets at War.* On the Front Lines. Mankato, Minn.: Capstone Press, 2004.

Hopkins, Ellen. *U.S. Special Operations Forces.* United States Armed Forces. Chicago: Heinemann, 2004.

Goldberg, Jan. *Green Berets: the U.S. Army Special Forces.* Inside Special Operations. New York: Rosen, 2003.

INTERNET SITES

FactHound offers a safe, fun way to find Internet sites related to this book. All of the sites on FactHound have been researched by our staff.

Here's how:
1. Visit *www.facthound.com*
2. Choose your grade level.
3. Type in this book ID **073686430X** for age-appropriate sites. You may also browse subjects by clicking on letters, or by clicking on pictures and words.
4. Click on the **Fetch It** button.

FactHound will fetch the best sites for you!

INDEX